The 5 Secrets of Employee Engagement

Randy Starr

DEDICATION

This book is dedicated to all the men & women who fight for our country, the first responders, the law enforcement officers and everyone who serves our country, states, and cities.

ACKNOWLEDGMENTS

I would like to acknowledge my family – they are simply awesome!
I would also like to acknowledge Gallup, McKinsey Global Institute, UNC Kenan Flagler Business School, Workplace Research Foundation and all of my connections on LinkedIn

THE 5 SECRETS of EMPLOYEE ENGAGEMENT

Employee Engagement...the Real Secrets

THE STORY

First, let me **thank you** for picking up my book and reading. Hopefully, you can follow me all the way to the end. I'm sure you're reading this book because you want to learn the secrets of employee engagement. I'm going to tell the story of how I discovered the secrets of employee engagement over the course of my career in the Hospitality Industry. Although both of the companies that I run now **RJS Data Group** and **5 Starr Engagement** focus on the Hospitality and Healthcare Industries, this book will transcend into any labor-intensive industry and assist you in increasing your engagement levels.

I will start this story with some background on myself which should help you understand why it took me so long to figure out the secrets to employee engagement. I grew up in a small town in West Virginia where getting a job at the local factory or chemical plant was the main goal of all my friends. Unfortunately, I followed this path for several years but quickly found out this was not my goal. I held numerous jobs in numerous industries in search of my career. I worked as a shipping clerk, a quick copy shop, convenience store, delivery person, waiter, worked on the labor gang, pipefitter, insulator, pipe welder, car sales, lawn care, and then I decided I needed to go to college. Out of all those positions I really enjoyed sales, so I thought that sales and marketing degree would be my goal.

RANDY STARR

You can probably tell from all the different positions that I held I was a little confused and wasn't sure what I wanted to do or how. One thing that was always in the back of my mind was owning my own business. Owning my own business was discouraged by my parents and my friends, it was too risky, and there was no guarantee of income or benefits. Regardless, I still wanted to own my own business.

All the jobs I held up to this point were either boring, extremely difficult, not stable or I just didn't feel like I fit as part of the organization. I had bosses that were, to say the least undesirable. When I was working construction, as you can probably imagine, not only were my bosses rude but they constantly harassed you to produce, which included yelling, threatening, and belittling. There were no work/life concerns, there were no wellness concerns, schedules were put out, and you are demanded to work the schedule regardless of your personal life. So, after a couple of years, I just grew to think this was the norm.

Since I didn't come from a family that was wealthy, I needed to work while I went to school. So, trying to find a job that would be flexible enough for me to both attend college and work were somewhat difficult, especially since the area jobs were mainly chemical plant or factory. I applied for many different jobs and during the interview process would determine that they would not be a fit for my current situation. One day I saw an ad in the newspaper for housekeepers at the local Marriott hotel, I thought if I could get a part-time job cleaning rooms then I could work around my school schedule and everything would work out.

RANDY STARR

THE REAL STORY

This is where the story starts – I went to the Marriott Hotel to fill out an application, I was greeted by the Human Resources Manager, given an application and asked to fill it out and bring it back to her when I was done. She was very friendly, professional and courteous – unlike anyone I have dealt with at work in the past. So, I was very impressed. She gave me a brief interview with all the typical questions and then told me that she would be in touch at a later date for an interview with the Housekeeping Manager. The next day I received a call from her to schedule an interview with the Housekeeping Manager, so I was very excited. When I arrived at the hotel, I was again greeted by the same Human Resources Manager and then escorted to the Housekeeping Manager's office. She introduced me to this gentleman and then left so that he could conduct his interview.

Apparently, the Housekeeping Manager was on his way out the door, meaning he was about to quit his job. The interview was miserable; he told me nothing but negative about the hotel, the work, and the company. I politely answered his questions and continued to act as if I was interested in working for him. Although, as I sat there I thought to myself I will never work for Marriott. I left the interview and drove home and told several people that not only did I not get the job, but I was not interested in working for Marriott. So back to the job search.

THE 5 SECRETS of EMPLOYEE ENGAGEMENT

Two days later I received a phone call from the Human Resources Manager; she asked me if I would be interested in coming back for a second interview. I told her that I had changed my mind and that I was not interested in working for Marriott; I can sometimes be very blunt. She asked me why I had changed my mind, so I told her that I was discouraged by the Housekeeping Manager and that he painted a very poor picture of the company the hotel and the job. She then explained that the Housekeeping Manager was no longer working there and that she had called me to come in for a second interview the Front Office and not the Housekeeping Department. They had a position open at the Front Desk for a part-time Front Desk clerk, and she thought I would be perfect for that job. She also went on to tell me that the Front Office Manager who would be interviewing me represented Marriott in a better light. I accepted and told her I was excited to meet the Front Office Manager and go through this new interview process.

I was told for this interview that I should arrive at the lobby not human resources department, inform the Front Desk that I was here for an interview and then have a seat in the lobby and wait for the Front Office Manager. This was very different as I walked to the front door and approached the lobby there was a gentleman standing behind the Front Desk with a big smile on his face surrounded by other employees who also had big smiles on their faces. I approach the gentleman introduced myself and said that I was here for an interview. This gentleman was the Front Office Manager;

he asked me to have a seat in the lobby, and he would be with me immediately. As he came out into the lobby, it was obvious that this gentleman was very professional and was also very enthusiastic about his job. During the interview which took about 45 minutes, he completely changed my mind about Marriott – I now wanted this job more than ever. He asked me questions about myself about my previous work history and about why I wanted to work in a hotel. He told me about the job the company and the hotel the entire time he spoke to me he was excited, enthusiastic and very attentive. We concluded the interview he told me that he had several candidates and that he needed to decide, he promised me that decision would be made within 24 hours and that he would notify me in the event I got the job or if he had decided to go with another candidate.

Those 24 hours were the longest 24 hours of my life, at that point. I was hoping that I had made a good impression on him and that he could see something in me that would make him decide I was the best candidate at that time. I woke up the next morning with nothing to do and found myself sitting around by the phone waiting for it to ring. I tried to occupy my time by continuing to search for a job, not having much confidence in myself at that point. Then the phone rang! – As I ran to the phone, I remembered that he told me he would call me if I got the job or if he was passing on me. I answered the phone with a bit of hesitation, the familiar voice of the Front Office Manager was on the other end, he said, "Randy! When can you start?" I told him I could be there in 45 minutes. He laughed and said that Monday at 7 AM would be just fine.

THIS IS WHERE IT BEGINS

He told me that I should park in the parking garage on a designated area where employees parked, that I should enter the building through the employee entrance and that he would meet me at the security desk at 6:50 AM. I thanked him and told him I would be there and was looking forward to the job.

I have always been a person who arrives early; I never want to be late. So, 650 AM meant I was there at 6:30 AM. I told the security guard that I was going to be met by the Front Office Manager at 6:50 AM. Just as I said that the Front Office Manager walked in the back door along with other employees. He immediately smiled stuck out his hand and said welcome to the Marriott. He then showed me the process for punching in for a shift, where timecards were kept, were the timeclock was located, showed me how to use the time clock properly, he explained what to do if I made a mistake, and who to contact. We then walked to the Front Office, and he took me into a room with a desk, computer and a chair. He asked me to have a seat and if I would like anything to drink coffee, soda or water. I must admit at this point I was so excited I didn't know what to do. This was so unlike any other job I have ever had in my life. This guy was my boss, and he was treating me like a friend. Something that I was not accustomed, but was liking very much.

Most of the morning was spent filling out paperwork, he sat beside me to make sure I had no questions, and that the paperwork was complete and correct. After the paperwork was completed, he took me on a tour of the hotel. This tour took me into all departments, all the different guest room types, back of the house, the kitchen, both restaurants, recreation area, and ended up in the General Manager's office where I was introduced to his administrative assistant and the General Manager. During the tour, I was introduced to every Department Head, every manager, and many employees. We stopped at the employee cafeteria sat down, had soda and discussed the tour. He wanted to know if I had any questions about the hotel or functions of the different departments. He spoke positively of all managers all employees all departments in the hotel and in general. After our break, he took me back to the office where we had filled out paperwork and explained that for the next several days I would be training on the computer in that office. He had already created a login for me and showed me how to log into the training and how to navigate through the entire training system. He then explained to me that he had several meetings that he needed to attend and introduce me to the PBX operator, and explained that she would be able to assist me if I needed anything during the training.

I sat down at the computer-based training and started my hotel career before I knew it the Front Office Manager was back in the office and told me it was lunchtime. He took me back to the employee cafeteria and showed me the process of getting your meal. He explained that if you worked from 7 to 3 PM you would receive lunch if you work from 3 PM to 11 PM you would receive dinner, and if you worked the night audit shift which started at 11 PM and ended at 7 AM you would get breakfast. That evening before I left the Front Office Manager came in with a handful of uniforms. The uniform consists of slacks and a shirt a blazer and a tie. He asked me to try them on to make sure that they fit properly and then explained that I would be required to be in uniform always from this point forward. He also handed me a shiny gold name tag which should be displayed on my blazer always. He gave me 3 shirts, 2 pairs of slacks, one blazer and one tie.

The next several days I went through the computer-based training until I had completed it and passed all of the tests associated with the curriculum. When I was done, I informed the Front Office Manager that I had completed the training and was ready. He laughed and said that there was still quite a bit of training left before I would be allowed to go to the Front Desk. I spent the next several days in the Reservations Department, learning how to answer a reservation call and input a reservation into the extremely complicated Marriott reservation system. After I was confident with that task and the Reservations Manager had given her approval, I then spent a day with the PBX Operator learning how to operate the switchboard, answer incoming calls, answer internal calls, transfer calls, and all the functions that are PBX Operator was responsible. Then I spent one day with the Engineer of the hotel, who mainly taught me safety and security. He explained how the fire system worked, what elevators did in case of an emergency, and what the Front Desk was responsible for during an emergency.

I trained for what seemed like months, but it was only 10 days. After all the formal training was completed, the Front Office Manager escorted me to the Front Desk. This is something that I will never forget; it was a narrow hallway that led from the back office to the Front Desk, the narrow hallway opened into this expansive lobby that was absolutely beautiful. This was the hub, the center, where everything started for a guest and ended for a guest. It was busy, there was a Front Desk Manager, a Front Desk Supervisor, and at least four Front Desk Clerk's attending to the needs of the guests and doing their daily tasks. I was a bit overwhelmed; I stopped at the end of the hallway...the Front Office Manager turned around and could see the fear in my eyes. He looked at me and said, "this is what you've trained for, you're more than ready, come on out."

He turned me over to the more than capable Front Desk manager, who then began showing me how and when to do certain tasks. See this was many years ago, before computerized hotels. Which means everything the computer does now, was done by hand at that time. Every time a guest made a phone call from a guest room we had to post that charge onto their folio, which was a 3-part document that logged all their charges during their stay. Every time there was a charge in the restaurant, gift shop, room service, health club, we would have to post these charges onto the guest's folio manually. This hotel had 354 rooms, two restaurants, a lounge which was "**the**" place to go. The Front Desk Clerks stayed busy for their entire shift; there was no downtime. Not only was this a rather large hotel it also maintained a very high occupancy rate throughout the year.

As I became confident and comfortable at the Front Desk I started to notice that there were many different occasions when the Front Office Manager would come to the Front Desk and hold impromptu meetings, these meetings were to keep us up-to-date on what was going on in the hotel. He would inform us of groups, functions, VIPs, etc. On a regular basis, he would read guest comment cards that mentioned employees throughout the hotel. He kept us informed of our overall scores; he kept us informed of the financial performance of the hotel. He was constantly bombarding us with information about our job. He constantly encouraged us to do better, if he noticed an employee struggling in any area he would schedule time with that employee to give additional training and counseling.

Not a day went by that I did not see him at work, he would always shake my hand and thanked me for the work that I had done that day. Anytime he noticed any of the employees going above and beyond he would find a time that day to recognize that employee in front of everyone at the desk. My coworkers came from all walks of life; some were young, some were old, some were male, some were female, we made up all nationalities. Yet he treated all of us the same. I must admit our performance levels were not the same; some were better than others, some strived to be better, some did not... But he treated us all fairly – he did not have a favorite.

I thoroughly enjoyed this job; I excelled at this job, I decided that this, the Hospitality Industry was going to be my career. I was given the ability to cross-train and work in other departments; I was given the ability to learn supervisory skills, I was given the ability to learn managerial skills, I was given the ability to learn anything I wanted to learn. Because of my eagerness to do better and grow within this organization, I was rapidly promoted. From a part-time Front Desk clerk to a full-time Front Desk clerk, from a full-time Front Desk clerk to the Senior Rooms Clerk, from the Senior Rooms Clerk to a Front, Desk Supervisor. After being a Front Desk Supervisor for about six months...I then made the inquiry – what do I need to do to become a Front Desk Manager? I don't know what they call it now, but then it was called the ID Program which stood for individual development. It was basically a three-ring binder about 4 inches thick full of tasks that you must complete, with each task being signed off by the Department Head responsible for that task. I went through this program in record time.

Another milestone in my career is when I had a meeting with the General Manager, the Resident Manager, and the Front Office Manager. This meeting was to offer me a position as a Front, Desk manager! The General Manager told me that he was hesitant to offer me this position because he knew I was in college and knew that me taking this position would mean that I would not finish my degree. He warned me and left the decision up to me. I asked for a 24-hour period to give my response, which was granted. I thoroughly went over the pros and cons of the different scenarios – and I chose to be a Front Desk Manager.

Choosing to be the Front Desk Manager and accepting this position meant that I was going to Marriott Corporate Headquarters, where all new managers went for Marriott Manager Training. This was my first official business trip. I would certainly have hundreds more in my career, but this one was very important. This was more of an orientation to Marriott Management than it was a training session. We spent most of the day at Corporate Headquarters learning about the company, getting a tour of the facility, and at one point we were ushered into an auditorium where Mr. Marriott himself came in to speak to us.

I continued to want to learn and grow as much as possible, with the Front Office Manager continuing to encourage me and point me in the right direction. I thoroughly enjoyed the new position. I enjoyed working in the hotel and serving guests; I liked helping solve problems, I loved the fact that there were many different people every day, I liked the team aspect, it was just a good fit... Really didn't think about it at the time, but I wonder why?

CHANGE...A GOOD THING

It was about this time that Marriott was developing a new brand; they called it Fairfield Inn. Marriott circulated internal advertisement for recruiting purposes. I got my hands on one of those advertisements, and one thing stuck out... It said being the General Manager of a Fairfield Inn was just like owning your own hotel. Could this be true? Is this the direction I should take? My friends and family couldn't believe I made it as far as I had now, so when I mentioned to them that I thought about changing from the Marriott full-service brand over to a new smaller "motel" brand called the Fairfield Inn, I was met with much skepticism. I mentioned to the Front Office Manager that I was interested in investigating this new brand and opportunities within it and of course he supported any decision that I would make that would help further my career. He suggested I contact the Human Resources Manager for the brand and request an interview. After driving back to Marriott Headquarters, in Bethesda Maryland, to interview for a position within the new brand I was met with a little bit of resistance. The Human Resources Manager told me that I needed more experience than I currently had, to make a move into the new brand. He explained that as the brochure had stated, this is very close to running your own business/hotel. He gave me an outline of all the areas I needed to work on and told me that once I had done that to give them a callback and he would interview me again for a position.

Returning to my hotel, I had a new goal. Complete everything on his checklist as quickly as possible, with sign-offs from the Department Heads that were responsible. This checklist took me about 90 days to complete, I contacted the Human Resources Manager for the Fairfield Inn brand and told him I'd completed the tasks, and they were signed off by all Department Heads and was now interested in interviewing once again for the position. He told me that would not be necessary that he had a position he wanted to fill in Charlotte, North Carolina and that I needed to drive to Charlotte, North Carolina an interview with the Area Manager and the Area Marketing Manager for that property. This interview went very well, and I was hired on the spot, accepted the position and moved to Charlotte, North Carolina to make a transition in my career from full-service Marriott Hotels to their new brand called the Fairfield Inn.

Just like all aspects of my job in the past this new job required additional training, I was sent to Detroit, Michigan to an already established Inn that was used for training new managers. I spent four weeks learning all the responsibilities, tasks, and philosophies of this new brand. After completing this training course, I return to Charlotte to my new hotel. Once again, I was fortunate to have a mentor who was concerned, caring and enthusiastic about everyone's job. Upon meeting my new manager, his first question to me was how soon would you like to be the General Manager of your own property? My answer was as soon as possible – so he said let's see how quick we can do it.

ALL BY MYSELF

Nine months later I was walking onto a construction site in North Carolina where they were building my new hotel...and I was the General Manager!

Once again this would require additional training, mentoring and lots of communication. My Regional Manager was a very professional individual who demanded and expected the best from all his General Managers. We got along great because I always did the best that I could in everything that I did... Whether I was successful, or I failed; I jumped in with both feet and did the best that I could. This hotel is in a location that at that time needed a quality hotel. We were so successful in this hotel that we broke records every quarter and continued to impress all that were watching. This was really my first opportunity to build and maintain a team to run a hotel. I had received such tremendous training and had witnessed this from my very first day working with Marriott, that it seemed almost easy to do. I was in a labor market that was incredibly beneficial to employers we ran an ad in the paper to hire 20 positions and had over 1500 people applied for those positions. We hired the cream of the crop; we trained them continuously, we treated them all the same, we recognized their contributions and kept them in the loop of everything that was going on. We respected them as employees and people. The hotel maintained a turnover rate of less than 10% for four years in a row.

THE 5 SECRETS of EMPLOYEE ENGAGEMENT

Shortly after the fourth year, I was notified that there was going to be some changes made in Marriott and at the hotel that I managed was going to be sold. I was also told that part of the "deal" was that existing management teams of these properties should remain in place, and no longer work for Marriott becoming employees of the new management company. I was crushed, this was overwhelming, devastating and very difficult for me to process. I had given everything I had to Marriott; I gave 110% or more every day I was at work, and they were going to sell me. The confirmation of this "deal" was delivered in a regional meeting by my regional manager; I broke down, cried like a little baby. It was embarrassing because all I could think of was all I had done for the company and now all of efforts and commitment were going to go away.

The company taking over the management contract of my hotel and 49 other Fairfield Inns across the nation turned out to be a blessing in my life. This company was run by men of integrity who had some, but not a lot of experience. They had big dreams; they were eager, they would do the work that it took, they had the vision to grow their company with major brands like Marriott and Hilton. I resented this company at first, because of my situation. As time passed and I got to know them and understand them, my passion and enthusiasm were reignited. The 50 General Managers that came on board helped this company create their culture. We wrote their Vision, Mission, and Values. We even help them create their logo, it was a fun company to work with, and we were all looking forward to the future.

Unfortunately, once again the hotel that I was managing was sold. Now I never claimed to be the sharpest knife in the drawer, but I was starting to see a trend. The new company that took over the management contract for my hotel was archaic. They owned and managed 20 personally branded properties that they built themselves and were quite successful. Apparently, Marriott saw something in them to grant them a franchise contract for this property; I was unable to see the same thing 90 days later I submitted my resignation. I went back to work for Marriott at another Fairfield Inn property in South Carolina, only to find out that this property was getting ready to be sold as well. At this point, I certainly see a trend and whether the employer was qualified or not this was not something that I wanted to continue. Moving across the country from one location to another as hotels sold was no longer appealing in my life.

STARTING FROM SCRATCH

This was when I decided to open my own business, RJS Hospitality Solutions. Since I've been in the hotel business for quite some time at this point, I had determined many services that were provided to hotels that were either inefficient or way overpriced. So RJS Hospitality Solutions, did just that - we provided solutions for the Hospitality Industry. Due to my extensive contacts in the industry, we were relatively successful right off the bat. We mainly focused on sales training and revenue management, however, after about six months I started thinking about developing a survey system for hotels to complete what was then called employee satisfaction surveys. This is where RJS data group was born.

I can remember back in my first hotel when I was hired as a part-time Front Desk Clerk one day the Human Resources Manager came to the Front Desk and said would like for you to come to the grand ballroom and participate in our satisfaction survey. I was impressed I was a new employee they invited me to give my opinions about my job, the company, and my work environment. None of my previous jobs cared at all what I thought.

I talked to numerous human resources professionals in the hospitality industry as I was developing a system for the survey process. I was fortunate enough to find several clients the first year and grew the business every year with quality organizations.

This is where it starts getting really good

When we first started doing surveys, everyone wanted them on paper, which meant that after the survey was over, we would receive boxes and boxes and boxes full of envelopes that were sealed and inside of each envelope was one survey. These surveys needed to be entered into a computer so that reports could be built, and clients could view them easily. This was a daunting task! In our office we had four rooms that were dedicated to data entry, in each room, there were at least four computers, and during surveys, all you could hear were fingers tapping on keyboards. Now, of course, surveys always include a comment question, back then this was a blank sheet of paper where you could handwrite your comments. Which meant that one of our data entry people would receive the survey and type into the system the comments that have been written. If you can picture the scenario that I have described I'm sure you'll agree that this could be a very boring task, data entry is not exciting. During our very first survey which was quite large, we had one gentleman doing data entry that would read some of the comments out loud. He was not familiar with the hospitality industry. Therefore, some of the comments he did not understand and some of the comments were just funny. I could hear these comments being read out loud from my office and eventually, they set up a whiteboard in the main lobby where they would write down the funniest comment of their shift and then wager with the next shift if they could come up with one that was funny.

THE 5 SECRETS of EMPLOYEE ENGAGEMENT

He shouted from the back of the room, "somebody has to do something about all these possums in the kitchen." I almost fell out of my chair laughing along with all the other data entry people in the room at the time. Of course, that one made it to the whiteboard and won the day. But it did something else at the same time; I started reading all the comments that had been entered looking for more humor. Some comments were short some comments were long some comments were positive some comments were negative, but I kept reading in search of humor. After reading every single comment for that client, I started to notice some trends. I didn't pay much attention to at first, but the more I read, the more it became obvious that this client had the same issues in all their hotels regardless of location, brand, or flag.

The next survey we did, I continue to read comments as they were entered… Again, looking for humor. Again, finding trends? These are the same issues from the previous client – but these were different types of hotels? As I mentioned before, I never claimed to be the sharpest knife in the drawer, so at this point, I wasn't really grasping the trends as I should have.

I've been reading comments now for over a decade – these comments come from every type of hotel. They come from resorts, full-service, long-term stay, focused service, boutique, all different brands, all over the United States, Canada, Mexico, South America and a few European countries. These comments all have something in common. Not that they were written or typed by hotel employees, but they all have similar or identical issues.

My first book, "employee engagement – what the hospitality industry is missing," is where I first started mentioning the five areas that were constantly trending in comments. I also started encouraging clients to incorporate questions that targeted these five areas. Unfortunately, some clients don't regard comments as highly as they do the quantitative scores. So, with both comments and scores to reflect a trend or need in these five areas was beneficial to everyone. I knew that these five areas were problem areas but still didn't recognize the fact that they were, "the secret." Again, knives in drawers.

THE 5 "SECRETS"

It wasn't until recently when I started looking back at my career and trying to determine why I was so engaged. Started remembering my first experience in the hospitality industry with the Front Office Manager and I started to see how the trends I had detected in comments were evident in my first experience but in a positive manner. So, could this be the secret? Could these five areas be linked to the reason an employee is engaged? I personally believe that if these five areas are addressed in your organization, you will create an atmosphere of engagement. It might not be the solution for everyone, but it certainly will be the solution for the majority.

Before we move on and I start to describe the five areas that I believe are the secret to engagement, I first would like to address engagement itself. We very commonly referred to employee engagement; which technically is correct but not accurate. What are employees? They are people! We are all people! Your goal is to engage people. We sometimes look at employees like they are a different type of person, but they're not. We also look at managers as if they're not employees, but they are. So, people engagement is what you're after – you want to engage the people within your organization regardless of the position that they hold. In a hotel you want the housekeepers to be engaged as well as the General Manager to be engaged. So, moving forward let's look at the engagement of people versus employees.

Here is a list the five areas or the secrets to engagement, think back about my experience when I first started working in the hospitality industry and see if you see the same thing I did – an obvious correlation.

Communication

I don't particularly see one of the five secrets being more important than the other, in fact, I see them as a whole being the actual secrets not individually. However, without good communication, the other four cannot happen. Communication in an industry such as hospitality or healthcare is vital, you have teams within teams trying to accomplish certain tasks with certain timelines certain expectations, and they all rely on one another to accomplish a mutual goal. If communication is lacking or if the communication is inaccurate, you will experience frustration, aggravation, and eventually disengagement. I was fortunate in my hospitality career to work for, and with some of the most effective communicators, I've ever met in my life. Communicators that understood delivering a message is only part of communication, receiving a message was the other part. Good communicators are always good listeners; they are not people who hear you, they are people that look you in the eye and listen to every word you say to gain an understanding of what you are trying to communicate to them. It is impossible to grow engagement within a team if there is poor communication or lack of communication. Highly effective teams rely on effective, thorough, and frequent communication.

THE 5 SECRETS of EMPLOYEE ENGAGEMENT

There are literally hundreds of thousands of books and articles written on communication, why would anyone be a poor communicator? If communication is vital to your success, which it is, take it upon yourself to evaluate your current communication style and effectiveness. If you deem it to be less than desirable, make a change.

I'm not sure if you'll be as surprised as I was to learn how many comments I would read from employees who mentioned poor communication. A lot of these comments don't come right out and say there's poor communication however they do indicate the lack of communication, lack of meetings, lack of huddles, lack of interdepartmental communication all of which falls under the communication banner – and should be addressed. I said 1 million times we live in a time where communication should not be an issue which should be in abundance, with all the different methods of communication from cell phones to emails or text messages to social media platforms why would we continue to have communication issues?

Looking back at the beginning of the book when I was describing to you my experiences in my first hotel, and healthy Front Office Manager bombarded us with communication this wasn't looked on as a negative, it was positive. By communicating to us the events that were going on in the hotel, the groups that were coming or going, the financial performance of the hotel this all made us feel part of the business or a part of the organization. I'm sure that there is the possibility of over communication, but I have not run into the hotel that has that issue as of today.

So, if you're looking for a communications system or plan to make sure that you are giving your people what they need, I would suggest that you just start with conducting impromptu meetings. Talking to a group of people on your team and give them information that's pertinent to their situation. Start doing that on a regular and frequent basis, and you will start to get questions for more information on different topics or different situations that happen on a day-to-day basis. Do not expect people to come to you to ask for communication unless they absolutely must have it to complete their task. You need to be the one who initiates the communication once you initiate the communication and open the lines it will then become a two-way communication or an actual conversation.

Once you have created the environment of conversation with all the people on your team you have moved into an area where the other for "secrets," will enhance the engagement of your people as well. If you are currently struggling with the people on your team that I suggest communication be the first "secret" that you attack. I would not suggest that you jump in with both feet and try all five "**SECRETS**" at once, let's focus on micro-improvements versus macro failure.

Training

Training should be a never-ending component of your organization. You should never stop learning, and you should never stop passing along your knowledge to the people on your team. Almost all organizations that I run across have some form of a training program, a formal training program that addresses all the required skills that your people should learn. This would be a great place to start. Make sure that all your people have gone through your formal training program. I was surprised to find out how many people are working in hotels and never got one day of training; remember back my first experience I didn't see a guest for 10 days. I had to know how to answer the phone, turn the fire alarm off, make a reservation, re-key a room, and give directions around town before I could even see a guest. Today we seem to have adopted the on-the-job training thought process, where the new employee shows up to work, and they're ushered out to the Front Desk or to follow a housekeeper on the very first day. Sometimes known as throwing them to the wolves. Please don't misunderstand me, I realize that everyone is busy, I realized that everyone has too many tasks on their plate, but when you choose not to train a new person on your team properly, you're just adding to the additional duties of everyone.

The lack of training of the people on your team is reflected in your financial performance, the service you provide your guest or customer, and most importantly the enthusiasm of the people on your team. Not to be overly dramatic but let's take this example; you have decided that you want to take up a new hobby and learn how to fly airplanes. Go to the local airport where they have a flight instructor who signed you up walks you out to the small single-engine aircraft tied down on the runway and says, "I know you have seen planes fly a lot on TV and you've probably even seen inside the cockpit, why don't you just take this one out for a short spin and bring it back and then we will go on from there". How would that make you feel? Obviously, that's not going to happen, because it's a life/death situation. What I'm trying to make you understand is the additional stress you add to a person when you put them in that situation of no training. They have zero confidence in their ability, and they're representing your organization and dealing with your customers/guests/patients, and they're not doing it in a positive manner. Oh, I know, you put a big trainee badge on them and think that covers it – wrong!

By not training your people, in the beginning, you're jeopardizing financial performance, service you provide to the customer, and the first impression of your new team member. When I break it down like that, hopefully, it makes sense and neglecting a training program is ridiculous. And that is just initial training, what about your ongoing training how is that accomplished? What about cross training? Are you allowing your people to train in other departments?

Ongoing training is vital to the continued success of your team because not only does it keep subject matter fresh in mind, but it just adds to their confidence. We live in a world of constant change so constant training should be used against or to combat that change. Again, I think you would be surprised to know how many comments I've read about the lack of training in hotels. Some of these comments even come from seasoned hotel veterans if you will, who come to you from another hotel. Often this type of individual is labeled or assumed that they know what they're doing. Do they know how to do it the way you want it done? Do they know how to do it the way your brand requires it to be accomplished? The only way to answer those questions is by training.

Cross training is an awesome opportunity for your people to gain knowledge, and if you think about it, it's completely a win-win situation. So, you have a housekeeper who has been cross-trained in laundry – one day the laundry person calls off sick; you have someone already ready to take their place. Let's say you have a housekeeper who is cross-trained at the Front Desk, and for some unknown reason your Front Desk person is scheduled to appear at 7 AM does not – housekeeper is already there, and can instantly take over. What's not to like about cross training? Why do so many organizations not cross training? I think if you adopt the philosophy of training all your people as much as possible, to the point where they may leave your organization, then you have done a great service for that person.

Respect

Respect breeds an engaging atmosphere. It is vital and found in all engaged workplaces. Respect is when you feel admiration and deep regard for another person once you feel that respect for another individual you demonstrated by showing you are aware that your employees are people who deserve your respect. You recognize that they have rights, opinions, wishes, experience, and competence.

There are many ways to demonstrate your respect for other people, treating them with courtesy and politeness and kindness is a very good start. One of the ways to demonstrate your respect for one of your employees is to ask their opinions frequently, especially when it has to do with something that will affect their job/work. Delegating meaningful assignments is also another way of showing your respect. All leaders encourage their teams to express their opinions and ideas. But, you must listen to what they have to say before you express your viewpoint. Don't cut them off in the middle of their thoughts; this is disrespectful.

Your team is made up of individuals that are doing the work; they know the job much better than you. Use your people's ideas to change and improve the workplace. Let your employees know you have used their idea, or better yet encourage the person with the idea to implement the change. Be aware of your body language and tone of voice the pitch your demeanor your expressions and all your interactions with employees. Your people hear what you're really saying in addition to listening to your words.

It is extremely important to include all your people in meetings, discussions, training, and any company events. I understand not every person will be able to participate in everything, but you do not want to exclude or leave anyone out. This is also very important that you praise much more than you criticize – this will foster an environment of recognition from one employee to another employee as well. It is also important that you do not judge, demean, belittle, or constantly criticize little things.

All leaders implement the golden rule at work – treat everyone the way you want to be treated.

Helping all the people on your team is another way of showing respect; make sure you don't discriminate and help only certain people. This is also a great way to open up the lines of communication. Just like the other "secrets," respect is an integral part of creating an engaged workforce. Just like the other "secrets" respect is also contagious, when you are respectful of your people they will be respectful of you and their co-workers as well.

Fairness

We've all heard the term, "life is not fair." This is a very true statement, mainly because what's fair to me may not be viewed as fair to you. Fairness is in many cases perception. My perception is my reality; your perception is your reality. It is very important to remember this as you go through your career. One of the most common comments that come from engagement surveys as it relates to fairness is about the work schedule. If you're honest with yourself, you will admit that you hate creating the schedule. Although a simple task, it is extremely difficult. Sometimes it seems like you can't please everyone, that is because you can't. However, it is very important when dealing with work schedules that you recognize the impact that the schedule has on the people on your team. You're basically telling them when they can spend more time with their family, more time away from work and do what they like to do.

Another topic that comes from comments that revolve around fairness is favoritism. Favoritism is toxic to the workplace; it can destroy unity, respect, and productivity. Nobody wants to work where they feel like their coworkers are favored over them. If you have ever had a boss who favored others, you can understand the destructive nature of favoritism.

It is important that you as a leader apply the rules to everyone in the same fashion, including yourself. If you take advantage of rules, then not only are you not being fair, but you are disrespecting your team. I frequently read comments about managers who do not apply the rules to themselves; for example, some organizations have a no cell phone at work policy. But managers, tell the staff that rule does not apply to them, how could that possibly be viewed as fair?

THE 5 SECRETS of EMPLOYEE ENGAGEMENT

It is also important that you are honest with your employees. Explain why procedures are in place, and why things are done a certain way. Don't just tell them that's the way it is, do it, because I said so. This will certainly earn you zero points, and be destructive to your efforts of creating an engaging atmosphere.

Don't confuse treating people fairly with treating people equally, this is very common and can create unexpected issues. Let me give you an example. Mary and Jane are two of your housekeepers, two very different individuals as all of your employees are. Mary works extremely hard every day, she goes above and beyond the call of duty on a regular basis. Jane works just hard enough to get her rooms cleaned in the appropriate amount of time. If you treat Mary and Jane equally, you could very easily create contempt in Mary's mind. Mary knows she works harder than Jane, as well as everyone else in the housekeeping department, so treating them as equals would not be fair.

I mentioned previously that fairness is a perception, so even if you are attempting to be fair, some will always not view you as fair. Admittedly, of all the "secrets," fairness is the most difficult to practice on a constant basis.

RECOGNITION

One of the basic employee needs is to feel like they belong or are a part of the organization...not just a number or another cog in the wheel. Recognition is a powerful tool that when used correctly can help accomplish this need. Recognition should always be done in public and does not have to be a formal program of awarding specific performance.

Some organizations have implemented formal recognition programs, like the Employee of the Month award. Some organizations track the number of days since the last accident. Some organizations recognize years of service by placing pictures of the employee on the wall listing their years of service. These are all good programs if administered correctly. I will admit that I have never been a fan of the Employee of the Month, for many reasons. Mainly, how is the employee of the month selected? Who selects them? What are the components of the selection process? In many cases it is a random selection made by a manager, this is a dangerous program when this happens.

What do the other employees who have been working hard think when they are not selected? Do you think that they work harder the next month in hopes of obtaining the coveted EOM award? In some instances, that would be true...but I don't believe that is what most employees do. If there is a known selection process based on many different performance components, and everyone has access to that information, so they can see what has determined the selection each month...then maybe it would be motivational.

The main thing to remember if you use a program that is not the only recognition you should be giving. In fact, you will find that informal recognition is more productive and less costly. When you recognize an employee in front of their peers for going above and beyond, you have just hit a home run! Of course, you would have to witness that act in person or be informed by another. When you thank an employee for their efforts, you are recognizing them...you are letting them know that you are aware of them, their job and the difficulties they face daily.

Small things make a big difference in the employee's life. When the supervisor or manager points out accomplishments on a regular basis and gives credit where credit is due, this type of recognition builds a foundation for engagement.

MAKING THE CONNECTION

I knew from my personal research that the 5 areas were important, due to all the comments that fell into these areas...but I did not realize just how important they were until I started trying to understand why I was such an engaged person. I spent countless hours trying to think of the reasons for my engagement, why I loved going to work, learning and trying my best to become better. One day all the pieces of the puzzle fell into place...it was the way I was treated. Now granted, I had not been treated very well in all my previous jobs, so when I got into an environment of engagement, it was like the difference between night and day. But my Front Office Manager was constantly using the 5 "secrets" to lead his team. At the time I did not notice or was I aware of his style of management. I decided he was a super nice guy who had my best interest in mind always. Now as I reflect upon those times I have determined how he accomplished administering the five secrets.

I have always encouraged leaders to spend time with their employees...some call it Managing by Wandering Around or Walking Around. The term does not matter, what matters is you are "in the trenches" with your employees. Observe everything, how they work, how they communicate, what they need and when they need it. This simple action will allow you to accomplish all 5 of the "secrets" at once. This is exactly what my Front Office Manager did so effectively.

THE 5 SECRETS of EMPLOYEE ENGAGEMENT

Rarely could you find him in his office, frequently you could find him at the Front Desk, in reservations, in the front lobby, anywhere where his team was located is where you could find him. He was required to attend frequent meetings with other managers and executive members of the hotel. However, when he was in these meetings we all knew where he was, and if we needed him, we could still contact him.

You see when the Front Office Manager was out and about in his areas of responsibility, he was working elbow to elbow with his team. He learned about his team he understood his team and he developed relationships. These relationships were developed by frequent and regular involvement in his team's daily activities. He took the opportunities to communicate to them as well as pass along knowledge that he had of their position. He treated everyone the same, respected everyone he met, and he constantly recognized performance. All his team members knew him, liked him, and trusted him, which is why he was so effective. These traits of his management style rubbed off on all of us; we constantly communicated we tried to help each other whenever we could we respected one another we were fair to everyone we also recognized each other. We all felt like we belong to a very special team.

HOW TO CREATE A STRATEGY

DETERMINE | GROW | MAINTAIN

While I was discovering the five secrets to engagement, I was also developing a system that would help organizations with their engagement strategies. I would like to share with you some of the processes that I have developed over the last decade, that will help you with all your engagement strategies.

The **Determine|Grow|Maintain** process or DGM has helped numerous clients grow their engagement quickly, efficiently, and cost-effectively. Of course, I would prefer that you use 5 Starr Engagement for this process, but I'm sure your current provider can also assist.

DETERMINE

Determining your current engagement levels is not as easy as just administering an engagement survey. An effective engagement survey requires that you develop a questionnaire that is focused on your organization's mission, vision, values, and goals. There are no "right" or "wrong" questions to ask, but if you are going to the expense and time of conducting an engagement survey, you need to make sure you are asking questions that "fit" your organization. The culture of your organization will determine many things, even the wording of the questions.

The survey should be scheduled for at least one month for everyone to prepare. In this case, preparation means promotion. We all know in real estate success is location,

location, location. Engagement surveys success is promotion, promotion, promotion! It is impossible to promote the "event" too much. A typical organization should start the promotion with notification to the field from the CEO. In this notification, the CEO should indicate the survey is an opportunity for all associates to communicate anonymously about their workplace, supervisor and management team. Anonymity is crucial for obtaining accurate and usable data. The promotion of the survey should continue within each hotel from the General Manager, department managers, human resources department, and supervisors. Take time out of your monthly all-employee meeting to promote the engagement survey. Take time out of your daily huddles to remind associates and give them the opportunity to ask questions about the survey. When you can be one-on-one with one of your associates, asked them if they have any questions about the engagement survey.

The timing of the survey is equally as important; you must give every employee the opportunity to participate and respond to the survey. The length of time the survey is open typically depends upon the number of employees you have in your location. I always suggest running the survey over a weekend or a payday, if pay stubs are distributed. You want to give everyone the opportunity to respond, regardless of the length of service. New employees have an experience that all employees probably don't remember or has changed since they were hired.

Method of determining engagement levels is also important. Do all your employees have access to a computer, tablet, smartphone... During the day? I have found over the years that this is not always the case. To make your survey more efficient, you may need to offer a conventional method such as paper and pen. Please be aware that paper and pen surveys typically take a few more days than a digital survey.

There are many things to consider when developing a new engagement survey, so make sure you give yourself enough time to create the questionnaire and schedule the survey properly. The last thing you want is to find out post survey one of your questions was incorrect. Once your survey is ready to administer it's important that you take several surveys yourself reviewing exactly what your employees will see when they respond to the survey.

Another consideration in developing your survey is the answer set or the potential answers your employees must choose from. I suggest the Likert scale as it is the most uniform and gives you the most comprehensive data. Typically, the Likert scale includes a neutral response... Meaning average. I've encountered several clients who do not like the neutral response and want to push the respondents into positive or negative. Their argument for this request is they do not want to be average but either want to be negative or positive, either giving them something to celebrate or something to work on. My counterargument would be average is something to work on.

GROW

You have finished your perfectly executed survey, and now you have the results! What do you do now? This is where most organizations drop the ball...not on purpose, but because they have little to no training in the "GROW" area of engagement. That is typical because they have no formal strategy...so the best of the best create Action Plans...others just look at their scores and wonder what they could do better.

Let's dive into the next steps. Review all data...gain a full understanding of reports and what they are telling you...and in some cases what they are not telling you. Hopefully, you have chosen a vendor that will first provide you with reporting that is easy to understand...like you have time to learn something new. That vendor should also be available to discuss and educate you on the reports when needed. The main thing is that you understand what the data is telling you. Once you understand where your engagement levels are in the many different areas of your survey, you can prepare to act.

Action plans are a great method for growing your engagement levels if the action plans are created properly. Unfortunately, in many cases, action plans are created by either the General Manager of the human resources director of the hotel, with no input from the people that they affect. Remember, earlier I mentioned one of the ways to show respect is to seek the opinions or input from people, especially if it affects their job.

Discovery Meeting – this is the method I encourage all clients to use to create action plans. A properly conducted discovery meeting will give you valuable insight into your need areas and at the same time give you an opportunity to celebrate and recognize the success areas. Depending on the size of your hotel/location Discovery Meetings can be and should be conducted in different fashions. For instance, a large full-service hotel with hundreds of employees should have discovery meetings conducted by the department. A smaller limited-service product can utilize in all employee discovery meeting.

The tone or atmosphere of the meeting is vital to the success. The purpose and goal of any Discovery Meeting should be to communicate the results of the recent engagement survey, then attempt to gather further information around need areas as well as celebrate the success areas. This is not a meeting of pointing fingers, accusing, or discounting the results due to a circumstance. The person conducting the meeting needs to be humble and ask for assistance from the employees. Get everyone in the meeting discussing the results. Make sure you ask questions of everyone, exclude no one. All of your employees have taken the survey, and now all should have the opportunity to discuss the results.

In many cases, the person conducting the meeting or the person in charge of engagement strategy attempts to correct too many issues at once. This typically results in failure, due to the overwhelming nature. Therefore, my suggestion is micro-improvement. First work on areas that appear to be easy to rectify. Then you will realize success is making ready to take on more difficult issues. If you can move your engagement a small amount every quarter, you will have made major changes in one year. It is much better to walk in the correct direction versus running the wrong way.

Discovery meetings that are conducted properly will result in a more unified team, and they will help you write the action plans. When the employees assist in the creation of action plans, they will also assist in the implementation, keep you up-to-date on the progress, and take ownership. This is exactly what you want. When the employees oversee action plans, they will get done.

The best way to determine if your action plans are moving the levels of engagement in the proper direction is to survey the people again. The frequency at which you survey should be determined in your engagement strategy. The frequency that you choose should be derived from your current level of engagement. Organizations that have high levels of engagement, a culture of engagement, and an atmosphere of engagement will probably only need to survey once a year. Organizations with lower engagement levels, are developing a culture of engagement, and are attempting to create an atmosphere of engagement should consider surveying at the very minimum twice a year. Some organizations that want to make a rapid, positive change in their engagement scores need to consider surveying every quarter seriously. At first glance, this may seem like an overwhelming or daunting task, but with the right partner, it should be no more difficult than one survey per year.

Once your engagement reaches your desired levels, you can then consider surveying less. But if you are attempting to grow engagement levels, how will you determine if your action plans are effective? A survey followed by implemented action plans followed by a survey is the recipe for engagement growth.

Over the years I have observed what different organizations do with the results of their surveys. I have determined, and mentioned some above, that there are certain issues that cause an inadequate action or no action at all:

- acting too quickly without the input of the team
- getting lost in the negative – dwelling on the negative
- discounting low scores due to certain situations (labor market, economics, etc.)
- focusing on the scores versus acting
- paying too much attention to comments versus quantitative scores
- "paralysis by analysis" – focusing so much on results and not acting
- taking results personally
- attempting to determine who wrote comments – "the detective manager."
- attempting to act on too many areas at once

Avoid these; engagement surveys are not rocket science they are simply a snapshot of your current engagement levels. As I mentioned before, it is best to thoroughly understand what the data is telling you and then act.

MAINTAIN

Maintaining your levels of engagement is as important if not more important than growing the levels of engagement. While you are focused on growing engagement in the areas that need growth, don't forget the areas that were successful – maintain them. On too many occasions organizations get focused on growing the poor results at the cost of the successful results. Continuous improvement is a term that comes to mind. You want to improve continually while at the same time not letting the areas that aren't currently being focused on slip.

Maintenance of engagement levels should be easy, just continue doing what you have been doing. This should also be part of your engagement strategy. I have only encountered ONE hotel in all the years of doing engagement surveys that did everything badly...so what you are doing well, continue.

Surveys are also a way to maintain...or at least determine if you are maintaining your desired levels of engagement. We offer many different plans to meet the varying needs of all clients, as it relates to the frequency of surveys.

YOUR ENGAGEMENT STRATEGY

Create a formal engagement strategy for yourself and your team. Educate yourself in the areas that you lack knowledge. Create a plan to improve yourself, especially in the 5 "secret" areas. This is not a personality overhaul; this is a skill enhancement goal. I know many different personality types that create tremendous atmospheres of engagement. The stoic and stern to the bubbly and relaxed...all can develop the atmosphere of engagement.

You may need to incorporate some of the "**SECRETS**" into your daily procedures. Make it a habit of doing a brief training and recognizing someone during your morning and afternoon huddle meetings. Evaluate the level of communication coming from you to the team, increase the communication...remember it is difficult to over communicate. Most people take communication the same way they do a grocery store...you only take what you want or need...the rest is left on the shelves...until they do need or want. Revisit your training programs, are they being executed to the best of your ability? Create cross-training programs for employees who want to take advantage.

There will be some changes in your current actions, but without change comes no change. These changes should be relatively easy to execute, and since they will be viewed as positive, you should get no kickback from your staff. Remember your team watches you always, and eventually, they will start to conduct themselves as they see you conduct yourself.

THE 5 SECRETS of EMPLOYEE ENGAGEMENT

Your strategy should include surveying as needed, at least twice a year until you are confident that your engagement culture is on cruise control. Action Plans and Discover Meetings are an integral part of your engagement strategy. Your strategy should be in writing, so everyone has access. Amend it as necessary, but get it started.

SOME NUMBERS

I have refrained from quoting statistics and results of years of monitoring engagement and its effect on organizations because I don't feel the need to "sell" engagement to you...you picked the book up with a need or desire to learn something about engagement. I do on occasions find myself educating people on the effects of engagement in a workplace...but not very often.

For those of you who do not know or possibly don't care:

According to **Gallup's 2017 State of the American Workplace** - Only 33% of American workers are engaged while at work. This, of course, leaves the majority not engaged or even worse – disengaged.

According to **The McKinsey Global Institute** – Productivity increases by 20% to 25% when employees are engaged.

According to **Gallup** – Organizations with engaged employees have 28% less internal theft.

According to Tower Watson – 57% of employees who said they were very stressed at work felt less productive and disengaged.

According to **UNC Kenan Flagler Business School** – Organizations with highly engaged employees had an average 3-year revenue growth 2.3 times greater than companies whose employees were only engaged at a normal level.

THE 5 SECRETS of EMPLOYEE ENGAGEMENT

According to **Workplace Research Foundation** – Increasing employee engagement investments by 10% can increase profits by $2400 per employee per year.

These are just some of the millions of statistics that revolve around employee engagement. The main reason why most organizations don't have the levels of engagement that they want or desire…nothing done after the survey…sorry, but if that is inaccurate, then it must be because they don't want to change.

RANDY STARR

ABOUT THE AUTHOR

Randy Starr has authored:
Employee Engagement – What the Hospitality Industry is Missing
Success in Today's Workplace – through 5 Starr Engagement
The 5 Secrets of Employee Engagement
He is also the CEO and President of RJS Hospitality Solutions, LLC
RJS Data Group
5 Starr Engagement LLC
Randy is available for engagement seminars, engagement strategy development, engaging culture development and of course employee engagement survey design.

www.ingramcontent.com/pod-product-compliance
Lightning Source LLC
Chambersburg PA
CBHW050243230526
45470CB00005B/2090